THE UNCONVENTIONAL WAY TO WEALTH

KNOW WHAT YOU DO NOT KNOW TO BE EXTRAORDINARY

REETU GOYAL KANSAL

ISBN: 978-93-95266-95-6 (Hardback)
978-93-95266-89-5 (Paperback)

Published by: Beeja House
Printed By: Repro India Pvt. Ltd.

First Printing Edition 2023
Author Email: support@reetugoyalkansal.com

MOTIVATE AND INSPIRE OTHERS!

"Share This Book"

MEET REETU GOYAL KANSAL
WHAT THEY SAY ABOUT HER
&
THE UNCONVENTIONAL WAY TO WEALTH

"Having known the author personally, I can attest to their unwavering commitment to helping others succeed. 'The Unconventional Way to Wealth' is a reflection of their dedication."

-- ***Sanjoli Aggarwal***, *MD Medicine, AIIMS New Delhi.*

"Kudos to the author for challenging conventional thinking. "The unconventional strategies in this book resonate deeply. It's not about being a part of rat-race but embracing your individuality to craft a wealth-building journey that's authentically yours."

-- ***Naveen Goyal,*** *Software Development Manager.*

"The unconventional strategies shared in this book mirror the way the world is evolving. It's not about fitting into a mould but creating your own unique path to financial freedom."

-- ***Shailesh Gupta***, *Managing Director, d.light India.*

Reetu's ability to blend practical advice with her methodologies makes this book a must- read for anyone who wants to become wealthy and is willing to take an unconventional approach. She has a knack for breaking down complex concepts into actionable steps lesser known to a majority of people, seeking to become wealthy and aspiring for a much better lifestyle.

"The Unconventional Way to Wealth" is a compass for people in the 21st century, and Reetu is undoubtedly a guiding force to let you stay on course in your journey to become wealthy.

-- **Chirag Kansal**, *Founder and CEO – RICH LIFESTYLE.*

"In a world obsessed with quick fixes, this book delves deep into a mindset shift that's essential for sustainable wealth. The author's concepts are like a compass guiding you toward sustainable wealth and success."

--**Vineet Kumar,** *Director – PC Modern School, Bhiwani, Haryana*

"This book redefines what it means to be wealthy. Its thought-provoking ideas encourage you to invest in yourself first, ultimately leading to a more fulfilling and prosperous life."

-- ***Manish Kathuria,*** *President and Business Head: Priority and NR Banking.*

"I am excited for the release of Reetu Goyal Kansal's book, "The Unconventional Way to Wealth". Their focus on personal growth and self-discovery aligns perfectly with my mentoring philosophy, and I believe readers will find their concepts truly transformative.

-- ***Shilpa Singh,*** *Life Transformation Coach.*

"I've had the honor of guiding Reetu Goyal Kansal on their path to success. Their book is a culmination of their dedication to exploring unconventional strategies that empower individuals to become the architects of their financial destinies."

-- ***Sami Wunder,*** *Dating and relationship coach for high achieving women.*

THE IDEAL COACH FOR YOU!

If you are ready to overcome challenges, have major breakthroughs, achieve higher levels, be extraordinary, wealthy and successful, then you will love having

Reetu Goyal Kansal as your Coach!

Contact – support@reetugoyalkansal.com

www.reetugoyalkansal.com

To Be Extraordinary, Wealthy and Successful!

To my wonderful son, Ruhaan, who gave me the beautiful experience of how it feels when two hearts beat together. Who taught me what unconditional love truly is and how it can change your entire world.

This book is an extension of our energy together. Your future is what drives me today.

Dedication

Since childhood, I have been possessed with the idea of living the best life I can ever imagine with an abundance of Health, Wealth, Love, and Happiness.

MANTRA OF MY LIFE

GOOD VIBES ONLY ...

I have always been a curious thinker, keen observer, dreamer, and admirer of life. I strongly believe, ***"Life Is Exactly What We Make with It".***

For me, life is magical and exciting. The smallest things about life are utterly delightful to me. Even after I have grown up into an adult, having many responsibilities, facing challenges, and overcoming difficulties I still have the same curiosity I had as a child. I still have the same feeling that everything is happening for my highest good and every day is a new day of life that promises more excitement and adventure. I still believe that the magic of life is real and everyone deserves to live the life of their dreams.

And today, I request every reader to take a few minutes out to acknowledge the wonderful ***"Gift of Life"*** they have as I do it while writing these beautiful lines about my wonderful and amazing life.

With a heart full of love and gratitude I am dedicating this book to my journey of life so far ...

DEAR LIFE,

I welcome you to be on the stage, to be in the limelight today and forever. You have always been the centre of my attention and attraction as I always wake up with excitement at what new you will bring to me today and every day. I have always been passionate about you.

Thank you for giving me everything I have asked and demanded. It's been a wonderful journey so far.

Thank you for teaching me so many things, giving answers to all my questions, and making me the person I am today.

I make sure to keep you as simple as you have always been for me and **I PROMISE** to make you even better every day.

On My Deathbed, I really wish you would grant me a few more days to live, for being such a wonderful human being who valued you and lived it to the fullest with high spirits, always welcoming and enjoying the twist and turns you have laid down for me to adventure, learn and grow from accepting everything as it is with full heart, flowing in the flow of you, always coming out of every challenge being stronger, more vibrant every time.

Without you and the lessons you have taught me throughout my life, I would not have the blessings of being where I am today.

Thank you for being such a wonderful teacher, friend, and companion!

Thank you from the bottom of my heart!

I love you dearly!

To understand life, you don't need any formal education but to learn from life experiences only.

A Message To You!

"No matter where you are in your life, what your current circumstances are, you can start from scratch", and create a life of your dreams full of health, wealth, love, happiness, and success."

This book, which I refer to as **"Wealth Guide",** is surely on its way to reaching the right audience, "You", who are achievers, active investors, corporate professionals with a growth mindset who want to create infinite wealth and success. Who wants to reach their highest potential and live life on their terms. Who wants to break free from the never-ending hustle of the traditional world and to create wealth and success on their own terms.

This book is designed to take you on a journey of increasing your

"Self-Awareness" takes you to a high level of consciousness, and sets you on the path to success in a way that you never thought of. It teaches you that ***"You Are Your Only Asset That Matters"*** and that you need to build and invest in yourself to create sustainable wealth. After all, if you do not invest in yourself first, who else will invest in you later? Unlearn the social conditioning, being the real, "authentic you", you do less and achieve more in life.

In this book, I am sharing with you the 5 Steps **"To Be Extraordinary, Wealthy and Successful".** All the new perspectives and positive ideas are designed to upgrade your consciousness and awareness about you only. It is a book that uncovers information that will allow you to unleash your Inner Resources.

Whatever That You Seek,
Is Seeking You Only.

This book is going to pleasantly challenge your traditional way of doing things and to get what you desire. It is going to show you an unconventional way to create wealth and success into your life.

It enables you to think and expand your mind to look deeply inside of you to find that hidden reservoir of Wealth that can shape your future and dream life. It contains all the deep insights and experience I have gained and learned about life, which is happening inside of you only.

This book will help you to know yourself better, who you are at your core and what is your true highest potential as a human being. It will certainly make you think deeply and pull you out of your comfort zone, opening your eyes and expanding your horizon so that you can see your real worth and true potential.

This book has the possibility to truly transform your life as you may start believing that you have all the powers within to create and manifest your dream life full of Health, Wealth, Love, Happiness, And Success.

The Only Field of Activity for You
Is Within Only.

You do not need to work on anything else but to work on yourself. The day you change yourself is the day you change your world. It inspires you to rethink and evaluate some of your most fundamental beliefs — the ones that hold the very canvas of your life in place, but which in fact may be limiting you. Anything less than Wealth and Abundance is a limiting belief.

It Is Your Birthright.

It does not matter which point and place you are at. You can start from scratch and build your empire of Wealth by being successful in your own unique and unconventional way.

This book also gives you the right map and directions. You adopt a new pair of lenses, glasses through which you look at life experiences, challenges, unexpected stops, detours, and turns from a very different perspective which makes this journey of life more interesting and adventurous for you.

It may take you some time to understand and follow the secrets unleashed and shared in this book but if you are ready to follow the path sooner or later you will become extraordinary, wealthy and successful. You will be enabled and empowered financially to do what you love to do, having ultimate time and money freedom. You will formulate your *Aim of Being,* learn the *Art of Investment* to create your reality and turn any of your ideas into gold.

Real Transformation Works from Inside Out.

Based on specific knowledge and awareness, implementing the simple yet powerful concepts I have explained in this book you can take your life to the next level towards becoming extraordinary, wealthy and successful.

This book has the potential to change your life completely and bring immense joy, wealth, and success into your life.

My Mission Is to Help You Unlock Your Wealth Potential, Direct Your Own Success Through Investing in Yourself.

Being Committed to Your Mental, Physical, Emotional Health and Spiritual Growth, Committed to Your Family, Desire to Make a Contribution to The Greater Good, To Be Engaged in A Cause Greater Than Self and Serving Your Higher Purpose.

When I Coach someone, I help them to learn more about ***"The Best Asset "*** that is you and unleash your true hidden true potential. This life journey that you are on is a gift and if you are committed to it then, go ahead.

Infinite Wealth Lies Within Only.

- *Reetu Goyal Kansal*

Contents

Dedication *i*
A Message To You! *v*

PART ONE : Introduction **1**

From Restriction To Ultimate Freedom

Return On Investment 3
Cost Of Ignorance 11
The Best Kept Secret 18
The Best ROI 21

PART TWO : Discovery Of My Life **29**

5 steps to Be Extraordinary Wealthy

Do The Inner Work 33
Define Your Aim Of Being 47
Shift Your Identity 57
Create Your New Reality 73
Unlock Your Wealth Potential 91

PART THREE : The Unconventional Way to Wealth **99**

Prosperity With Peace

Trinity Of Wealth - Within 101
Invest Your Time Wisely 117

Acknowledgements 123
About the Author 127
References 134

PART ONE

INTRODUCTION

FROM RESTRICTION TO ULTIMATE FREEDOM

Return On Investment

Portfolio of Life

Return on Time Investment was the structural thought that first led me to outline the framework of this book. I was conscious of investing my money but I was never conscious of investing my thoughts, energy, and time. I was not aware of what kind of return and results I would be getting from the time investment that I have committed to. I was not mindful of where I spent my time, my thoughts, and most importantly, my attention and energy on a given day.

Was I aware of my own thoughts and feelings? Was I aware of my purpose and the importance of my existence on this planet earth? Was I aware of my values, worth, and potential as a human being? The answer was a simple **"NO".**

I was not investing myself consciously but spending my thoughts, energy, and time in all the different areas of life and as a result, I was not able to create the life that I wanted to create. I was close yet it seemed a distant reality.

Simply put, no one wants to spend but to invest their money, time and energy into something that does yield a decent return.

So, I had to go through this entire journey of self-discovery and re-thinking my life portfolio considering this important aspect — ***What is the Return that I was getting on my time and energy investments?***

Let me tell you more about my life Portfolio before I started investing in myself and diversifying my identity in all different aspects of life.

Being an adult and joining **"The Rat Race"** I always chased something more to achieve — more money, more security, more stability. Being a part of this never-ending cycle of searching for the next thing, I was being focused on doing my **"Best Work"** instead of being my **"Best Self".**

And then, I realised that in this process of achieving more, I had started losing many important aspects of my life along the way. I observed some down trends in all areas of my life — physical health, relations, career and finance.

I was not aware and conscious of such losses can cause one to become resentful and lose parts of what made you unique.

I felt lost and I was looking for clarity. It felt like things were at a standstill. I was searching for answers and did not know where to find them.

I started feeling exhausted, tired, and burned out. I experienced a poor "***Work-Life Balance***" and my life portfolio was sinking. It was not aligned and definitely, it was not one of the best life portfolios I ever wanted to have.

This phase of my life gave me enough reasons to conduct a "Root Cause Analysis" of this life escalation. I became curious and wanted to know where I went wrong. What could I not see or overlook? Why was life treating me the way I did not deserve? I wanted to see myself back in one piece again and to solidify what made me leave those pieces of me left behind in the first place.

This was my wake-up call as I was not feeling fulfilled, or making a difference even after doing so much in life, almost everything I have been taught to do.

All of these questions took me on a path of Personal Growth and Self Development. I used this challenging phase of my life to search for and seize the hidden opportunity.

"Some Beautiful Paths Can Not Be Discovered Without Getting Lost".

- Erol Ozan

The advantage of losing something is that it can always be found again. With this strong desire to find solutions to all the challenges I was encountering in my personal space, I entered this unexplored, unknown realm of the ***Inner World*** and received immense knowledge which transformed me completely and made me who I am today.

I became so passionate about diving deep and finding the root cause, I started enjoying this new journey of ***Self Discovery!***

"Blessing in Disguise", A natural way of giving you something by making you uncomfortable.

I realised that being an adult, I prevent myself from continuing to enrich my life. I forgot to continue to invest in myself.

I forgot about my early days in school, college, and university. They provided me with the skills to be in a position to earn an income.

There is no second thought that earning income is important but self-investment is the foundation on which everything else is built.

While education is a necessity as a child, it is still a form of investment. However, I got subscribed to the idea that an investment is something that is expensive. The truth is that an investment is something that has value and does not necessarily mean it is expensive.

I started reading books again, taking time to improve my health, learning how to manage my emotions and taking time to learn yoga to relax and meditate through day-to-day frustration and challenges. I started following mentors for advice, learning new skills, educating or upgrading myself.

This whole journey of finding myself back and investing in self-led me to such discoveries that I found amazing things about myself. I started doing things I have never tried and was not even aware of my true potential.

I found myself as a new person, completely transformed. I used to give deep thoughts and focused my mind on real-life situations, but this phase of life has activated my ***Inner Intelligence*** which gave me courage, time, skill, focus, and determination to write this book which I have never thought of in my life.

I have found that ***Inner Path*** to create whatever I want to create in my life. I found that everything that I was seeking in the outside world was actually lying within me only. And that made me realise and believe in the powers that I have. What I also realised was that, although I experienced a great loss of clarity in the beginning, I ended up gaining a new and improved Life.

"Growth Comes from Chaos, Not from Order".

- Chirag Kansal

What This Means to You is that when life throws multiple challenges, adds responsibilities, shatters your strong rooted beliefs, and gives you a cultural shock, when it becomes off-centre sometimes, it is very obvious and natural that you get lost with no clarity of your goals and what to do next in your life.

- You feel you are working really hard to achieve your goals, you feel your energies are scattered and getting eroded day by day.

- Your "TO-DO" list appears to be the size of the empire state building and still feel that your true potential is not being utilised.

- You may feel you are very busy but not sure you are accomplishing anything. You feel stuck.

- You feel burned out. You are constantly tired and have headaches or other physical, mental, and emotional signs of stress, frustration, and exhaustion.

- You feel like you are living someone else's schedule, taking multiple actions without the right direction, and have lost all your powers having no boundaries at all.

- You are feeling overwhelmed as you may have multiple responsibilities to your family, your work, your children, or your community. They are all competing for your valuable attention.

- You do not have the freedom to live and express yourself freely, you feel helpless.

- Even after working so hard, and devoting many years of dedicated effort, life still feels empty. Success, happiness, and satisfaction are still things to accomplish in the near future.

- You are living an ordinary life and nowhere close to being extraordinary.

All of this is very normal to feel and experience this way, when challenging situations appear in life. But they appear in order to help you to come out of your comfort zone to grow, to develop higher qualities, virtues, skills, knowledge, and experience you must have, and you must change the way you view things.

In this way, every setback, frustration and challenge, obstacle and struggle — becomes a positive and powerful lesson for you!

Every coin has two sides to it. There is a bright side to the darkest circumstances. There are no mistakes but lessons. There is no such thing as a negative experience, only opportunities to grow, learn and advance along the road of *Self-Mastery.*

Get in ***The Driver's Seat*** and travel in your own unique way. Let your Goals and a map guide you, and be open to unexpected detours. Do not be afraid to step outside your comfort zone. Enjoy this roller coaster ride of your beautiful life.

"From Struggle Comes Strength
and Pain Can Be a Great
Teacher."

- Robin Sharma

Cost Of Ignorance

Root Cause Analysis

For 33 years of my life, I followed everything, I have been taught by our education system, teachers, friends, family, society, media, government, and religion. Being in complete alignment with the outside world, I always put my best efforts to make a difference and to reach my ultimate goal of becoming ***Extraordinary Wealthy and Successful.*** I have done everything starting from:

To Study Hard
To Get Good Grades
To Get a Good Job
To Work Hard
To Earn Well
To Get Settled in Life
To Get Married
To Have Kids
To Chase Success...

But I was disillusioned in this pursuit of Happiness, Growth, and Success and was unaware of my own Needs, Desires, and Feelings. I was being ignorant of myself.

Growth was always measured by a grade or a salary and I was never taught the importance of self-love, growth and personal development.

Over a long period of time, I was unaware of the fact that I was the most valuable asset of my life. I was the type of person with a tendency to put others' needs above my own. I paid a lot of attention to how others felt at the expense of my own feelings. I spent a significant portion of my life focusing on others and taking care of their needs and desires, helping my friends, family, colleagues, and others. I was neglecting my own individual needs. I was being ignorant and the Cost of Ignorance was actually costing me my time, money, values, and above all, it cost me my happiness.

This unconscious, ignorant, and selfless lifestyle was not a healthy way to live and it was causing me to experience near-constant burnout.

I have been conditioned to believe that grades, salary, and status are the main things that bring to us everything that we want in our life.

Unfortunately, our education system does not teach us anything of this sort based on the overall development of an individual's physical, mental, and spiritual development but focuses more on building the IQ so that we can earn money and gain materialism for survival. No doubt, money, and materialistic things are needed but not to the extent that we forget to learn our true nature of love, compassion, care, and help for others.

No one is taught that the "I CAN" is more important than "IQ". No one is taught the power and true value of *Investing in Yourself.* No one is taught how to master their own being, thoughts and emotions. Thus, accept and love ourselves as we are.

What This Means to You is that growing up you would also have been taught to get good grades so that you can attend a university, attain your degree, and find a job that pays well. You have probably subscribed to this life and become disillusioned with where it has left you. And most people in the pursuit of *"Satisfaction & Contentment",* end up paying off student loans, paying off home loans, investing in a property that cannot be maintained, drowning in debt, and remortgaging credit just to survive. You have been trained and taught that you have to fight to survive. And This is ***"A Survival of The Fittest World".***

As a result, you are always competing with others, with your parents, with your siblings, with your friends, with your partners, and with yourself.

In reality, whosoever is aligned with the outside world is unaware of who they are, no one is satisfied and close to creating their *Dream Life* of health, wealth, love, happiness, and success. No one is even close ***To Becoming Extraordinary Wealthy and Successful.***

But let me tell you one thing: the people who are Wealthy and Successful in every aspect of their lives — the ones who you aspire to be — tell you that self-investment is the key to a balanced life, free from all distractions.

What I have learned through all the different experiences of life I have gone through is to reverse this cycle and start investing in myself to prioritise my Personal Growth and Self Development.

Self-Investment Is The Acknowledgement Of You As An Asset.

It is great to help others, to be kind but this can never happen at your own expense. I needed to take responsibility for my happiness first, I needed to satisfy my own needs and invest in myself first and foremost.

Ignoring Self and Expecting to Be Extraordinary, Wealthy and Successful, Isn't It Contradictory?

While Working with The Banking and Financial Industry, I Have Learned That in A Financial Portfolio, Money Is Invested in Different Assets to Minimise the Risk and Maximise the Return.

Diversification ensures that even if one asset is suffering, you have other assets that might over-perform. Thus, you reduce your overall risk and maximise value.

And when I applied the same learning and diversified my life portfolio, I felt happier, fulfilled while being aligned with my life purpose.

I invested in myself in such a way that I followed my unique path to have it all in every dimension of life, without sacrificing anything that truly matters to me.

Let me also give you a glimpse of my ***Life Portfolio after*** I started investing in myself and diversified my identity in all different areas of life.

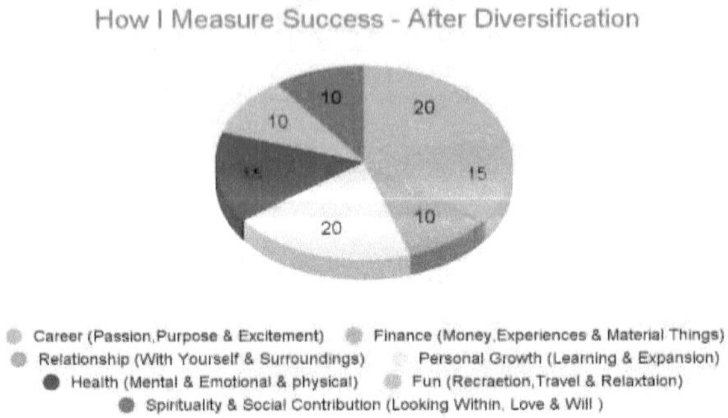

What This Means to You is that you must constantly be striving to improve the quality of your life keeping in perspective all areas of your life. Even though your success is not guaranteed. Eventually, you will grow as a person and it increases your chances of succeeding manyfold.

When you choose to invest and grow in all different areas of life, it keeps you afloat when one part of your life is not going according to your plan.

Always remember only your work is not your complete life. It is an important part of your life. but it is just a part of the whole pie.

Invest in your personal growth, do what you love to do, build your brand, create your niche in the market, learn new skills, and take care of your mental, emotional, and physical health. Build a strong relationship with yourself and your surroundings. Have fun while contributing socially and progressing on your spiritual journey towards reaching your highest best potential.

Draw the wheel of your life having a clear vision in your mind. Be more mindful of where to invest your time and money, and most importantly, align your thoughts and energy on a given day and at a particular time.

You can never go wrong with investing in yourself. That way, everything that you learn and you have can go with you. Invest in yourself through gaining wisdom, and knowledge, apply that knowledge, and never ever stop learning. **Be a long-life learner.**

He Who Stops Learning and Investing in Self Is a Dead Person.

The Best Kept Secret

Invest & Reinvest in Yourself

You might have heard the phrase ***Invest in Yourself.*** But what does it mean exactly and how can you go about investing in yourself? When you think of investment, most of you probably think of buying stocks, shares, and property.

But investing in yourself is a bit different. It is the ability to invest your energy, time, efforts, and perhaps a little bit of money into enhancing, nurturing, and growing your mindset.

The best kept secret of all wealthy people is to ***Invest and Reinvest.*** Their focus is not on spending, having liquidity, cash, or traditional savings, but on the constant growth of their assets, and they also have the wisdom to know that they are their only true asset.

Self-Investment might require your money, or time, or both, but the return is far greater than anything monetary. There is no risk involved, and you get out several times what you put in.

What This Means to You is that Self-investment allows you to develop every aspect of your life by targeting your skills, developing your talents, and giving you the clarity needed to navigate the obstacles in your path. You will begin to become a High-Value Self, a High-Income Earner who thrives in every aspect of life.

Trust me, you are currently performing at a quarter of your true potential. Once you start Investing in yourself you will see your true self-worth.

Investing in yourself and taking care of your needs is an active process, which requires constant attention, and therefore high profit and dividends are yielded.

Self-Investment means you choose yourself, observe yourself and decide which parts of your daily habits and thought processes need to be discarded as well as which parts need to be nurtured and invested into which allow you to Become Extraordinary, Wealthy and Successful.

It instils ***An Investor's Mindset*** in you, helping you to understand that income can be made from all sources if only you are open to all sources of income. A person who does not understand the power of Self-Investments and who does not continue to invest in themselves begins to build a life on a foundation that is not solid.

Therefore, the best time to start investing in yourself is right now. When you bank on Self-Investments, you are sure to increase your value, you are sure to increase your worth too.

Self-Investment Is the Only Guaranteed Investment One Can Ever Make!

The Best ROI

Low Risk -High Yield Investment

Investing externally, in other people, or in other assets may yield high profitability but self-investment is always the lowest-risk and high-yield investment.

What This Means to You is that your unique skill sets and talents are worth investing in; they are assets that will never decrease in your life. When you purposefully work on yourself to grow and glow as a better person do not think of it as an expense, instead, it's an incredible investment that you are making.

Once you embrace the idea of constant upskilling and utilising your unique skill to yield high returns and results, you see the real value of investing in yourself. The need to invest your time, thoughts, and energy into the right place will be greater than. The benefits that you reap can be personal or professional or could simply be a way to achieve your goals in a way that creates mindful satisfaction.

Self-Investment is going to give you the return that you want. Irrespective of the external environment and circumstances, it determines what type of life you live and what type of future you hold.

It does not need to be a grand affair, simply half an hour a day, you follow the morning rituals, seek wisdom, pursue knowledge, and grow in your skill is enough to make a change and to bring a difference in your life. Putting these new skills, you learn into practice means your investment is paying off.

Self-Investment May Not Necessarily Mean to Be Something Expensive.

Self-Investment acknowledges you as your only asset and it sets you on the path to reaching your full potential.

As you invest in yourself, you ensure you have more money than you need. You build more assets that work for you rather than liabilities working against you.

- **YOU DISCOVER AN UNCONVENTIONAL INNER PATH TO BECOME EXTRAORDINARY, WEALTHY AND SUCCESSFUL.** Maximising time and energy are the greatest asset any person can build for themselves. Very often people sacrifice certain aspects of their lives to fill a need in other areas. Investing in yourself forces you to take a look at every area in your life that needs improvement, and insists you build more assets for yourself than liabilities.

- **YOU GAIN CLARITY TO FORMULATE YOUR AIM OF BEING.** As you begin to invest in yourself and peel back the layers of your inner existence you become more aware of yourself and you become clearer on your priorities. You are able to set clear and defined goals for yourself. Goals that are purpose-driven and followed with passion are more attainable because you have discovered your purpose. You become aware of the path you are meant to follow. You no longer follow others, you trust your intuition to guide you, and your tenacity to see you through any obstacle.

- **YOUR INSPIRATION COMES FROM INSIDE AND YOU FEEL INSPIRED MORE THAN EVER BEFORE.** You begin to achieve your goals as you become more aware that these goals exist somewhere within you only. You see your path and the end results more clearly. You begin to prioritise your development over anything which is meaningless and can be defined as a time waste. You begin to feel this need to be more productive and efficient in your daily life to bring better change and automatically this reduces your daily distractions and clouds of negative judgement of yourself.

- **YOU TAKE INSPIRED ACTIONS BEING IN ALIGNMENT WITH YOUR HIGHER SELF.** As you grow, develop, become more mindful, and in tune with yourself, you begin to learn more about your inner self. You become more aware of your shortcomings that you may need to overcome. You become more aware of what your true abilities, aspirations, and inspirations are. You begin to uncover what you value in life and how your belief system influences the decisions you make. Your purpose begins to become clear to you on a professional and personal level. You take the inspired action of unfolding the state of your higher purpose.

- **YOU HAVE YOUR POWERS AND ENERGIES BACK IN YOUR CONTROL, YOU FEEL EMPOWERED.** When you are more aware of yourself, your personal relationship with yourself and others will improve and your career prospects will broaden. Self-investment develops your self-awareness, emotional awareness and broadens your career knowledge and skill set too. It becomes easy to control your negative emotion and you become more conscious of behaviours in yourself and in others that require nurturing. You develop the ability to distance yourself from any toxic behaviour that may be causing you harm and you learn the skills to communicate your viewpoint as well. Investing in yourself is the key to opening the door to your dream positions in every area of your life being wealthy and successful.

- **YOU RECEIVE REWARDS IN ALL AREAS OF YOUR LIFE.** Self-investment puts you in charge of your own destiny by showing you that knowledge and skills can be acquired by anyone. Awareness of your uniqueness, and your inner talents, along with the acquired knowledge and skills give you the extra edge. Investing in yourself boosts your confidence to put your uniqueness on display, making everyone sit up and notice you! You become the best version of yourself and reach your highest potential. It boosts your morale and your ability to achieve anything you set your mind to and this makes you feel fulfilled.

- **YOU LOVE AND ACCEPT YOURSELF, AND YOU FEEL FREE.** Self-investment increases your emotional awareness. You become more aware of your energies. You learn to pause and you no longer react but respond to any situation. It helps you to sail through your energies in motion, seeking to solve an issue rather than becoming engulfed in the negativity it creates. When you have a great sense of self your coping mechanisms are far better, your higher faculties are under your control and you know when to walk away when to offer constructive advice, and when to accept constructive criticism. Self-investment also teaches you to go with the flow as problems are inevitable parts of life, these contrasts are your "North Star "for you to be on your path of *Becoming Extraordinary, Wealth and Successful.*

Self-Investment Is the Key to Create Sustainable Wealth.

-Reetu Goyal Kansal

Self- Analysis Test Questions

- Do you have a diversified life portfolio?
- Are you not paying the cost of self-ignorance?
- Do you invest in your personal growth & development?
- Do you feel worthy and wealthy enough with all your traditional investments?
- Do you feel you have reached your highest potential?

- Do you feel you have become the best version of yourself?
- Do you feel you are the extraordinarily high value individual who is creating infinite income, influence and impact?
- Do you love what you do?
- Do you have time and money freedom?
- Do you live life on your own terms?
- Do you serve your higher purpose?
- Do you have clarity of what you want and who you are?

If the answer is "YES", then you can stop reading the book right away but if the answer is "NO", you are at the right place, at the right time reading the right book.

"You Are About to Know What You Do Not Know to Be Extraordinary, Wealthy and Successful".

PART TWO

DISCOVERY OF MY LIFE

5 STEPS TO BE EXTRAORDINARY WEALTHY

5 STEPS TO BE EXTRAORDINARY WEALTHY

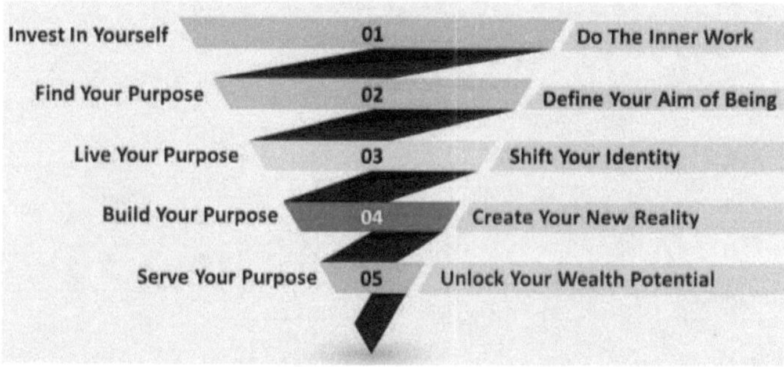

"A man travels the world over in search of what he needs, and returns home to find it."

–George Moore

Do The Inner Work

Invest In Yourself

The First Step Towards Being Wealthy

UNLEARN SOCIETAL CONDITIONING

Inner Work is something that is necessary and simply the process of deconditioning and unlearning everything you are taught, and conditioned to believe, see, feel, and understand in one way or another.

In life, you go through so many things that consume your energy and attention. All of these things shape you in one way or another. And if you lack Self - Awareness you have no or little control or real direction in your life.

To be able to understand yourself better, experience more joy and less suffering, manifest and create the life you truly want to live, passionately fuelled by your heart's desires, you have to find the courage to empty yourself and be willing to face your inner self. You are a profitable prospect and what lies within you matters.

Inner work is the key to higher self- awareness, which helps you to understand yourself better, find your true calling, unique path and purpose.

It is a matter of personal hygiene and it demands learning, educating ourselves with real knowledge, and researching. It is like entering your ***Inner Laboratory*** and understanding the complexity of emotional depths (your energy wheels), your nature of existence, the human soul or mind.

An entirely new set of reactions, a change of consciousness, your re-birth, and your real transformation depends on your inner work.

Once you begin doing *"Inner Work"* you have to change your whole approach the way you think, and restructure your thought patterns.

See the connection between the outer experience and the inner thoughts not to remain a victim in your life. You have to invest your energy directly, not in any person, or anything, outside of you. The essence of our enjoyment comes from the inside. It is your ***Inner State*** that attracts your outer life. You are surrounded by true images of yourself.

What You Are, That Only You Can
See.

What This Means to You Is That Doing the *Inner Work* and Observing Yourself Would Reveal Your True Inner State.

To What Thoughts Are You Consuming?

With What Feelings Are You Identified?

With What Actions Are You Consenting?

Self-observation would reveal the deceitful one in you; and this must be accepted before there can be any real transformation. At this moment try to notice your inner state — your patterns, programs, hidden fears and unconscious desires. Notice your emotions, habits, or thoughts that recur. Do they help or hinder your growth?

Most of you think that you are kind and loving, generous and tolerant, forgiving and noble- but an uncritical observation of your reactions to life will reveal a shadow self that is not at all kind and loving, generous and tolerant, forgiving and noble. And it is the self you must accept and then set about to change.

Your mission is to embrace it all, to integrate all parts of your existence, to accept the whole of your being, and to accept all that you see, feel, experience, witness, imagine and dream. and for that, you must be very careful of where you are within yourself. it's you that must be changed.

There is an *Inner You* that you must first accept and then set about to change. But if you are unaware of your true Inner Self, you are stuck in one melody, you keep repeating the same track and there is no way out.

A life full of Wealth and Abundance, does not begin with external possessions and accomplishments. This perception is simply a result of the current society model, but it does not serve your highest good. What you truly desire deep within begins deep within.

My intention of writing this book is to help you become extraordinary, wealthy and successful that lies within you only. The activities in this book will take you through some deep Self-Realisation and it is going to help you build a deeper and stronger connection with your higher self so that you can start this inward journey, the process of unlearning what is no longer serving you and finding new paths that are meant just for you.

Simply allow yourself to dive deep inside yourself, somewhere quiet and peaceful where there are no distractions, and go through this book without judging yourself, but accepting yourself fully and completely understanding that you are a work in progress.

Complexity is intricate only until you realise how simple it actually is, so do not get worried or frustrated by not getting there immediately.

Inner Work is not something that is meant to be easy or something quick. Have patience with yourself while doing your *Inner Work* and finding who you are within yourself. For it is the sole cause of everything you observe.

Your description of the world is a confession of the self that you do not know.

You describe another - you describe society- you describe anything- and your description of the thing you observe reveals to one who knows this law of being you really are.

You have to be patient, understanding, open-minded, open-hearted, forgiving, ready to learn from others, ready to listen to other sides of the story, ready to release all that you have learned so far, and ready to face your *Inner Self* no matter what!

Accepting the self that needs to be changed will create space for you to experience a new version of you. You just need to be open and speak your intention of being as an awake, true, authentic and authoritative self to receive your desire to be extraordinary, wealthy and successful".

Look within and you will have
everything that you seek outside.

- Reetu Goyal Kansal

INNER WORLD V/S OUTER WORLD

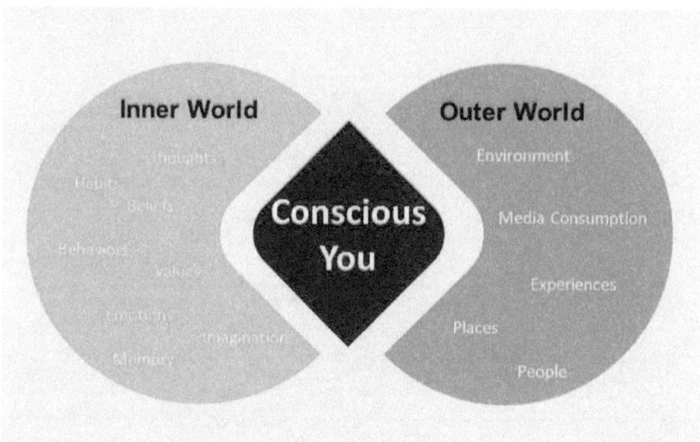

Everyone has a rich ***Inner World*** but no one pays attention and runs the risk of going through life on autopilot.

Your *Inner World* is everything that happens in your mind such as your thoughts, memory, feelings, beliefs, core values and desires, imagination, etc.

Whatever is happening inside, you see the physical manifestation of it outside.

Under the influence of social conditioning, you never understand why you do what you do.

You do not even realise the potential that you have for greatness. The outside world and the external assets you focus on building, cannot give you everything that you want.

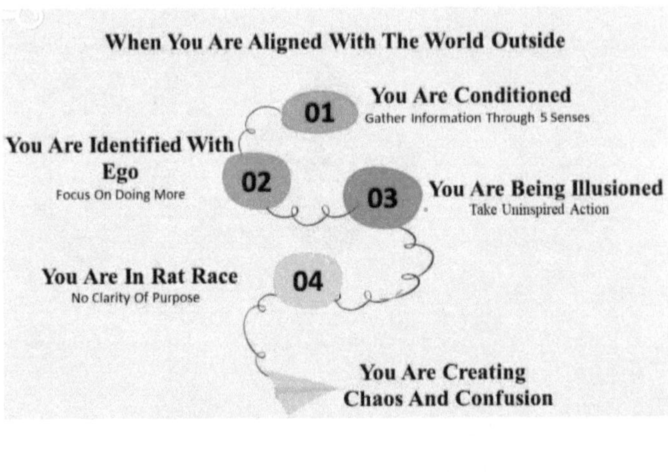

"Do Not Be Caught Up with The Outside World, Pay Attention to Your World Inside."

Do not try to achieve anything by focusing entirely on the outside world forgetting that you can only create your dream life full of health, wealth, love, and abundance when you go beyond the unseen where all the answers lie in your *"Inner World".*

What This Means to You is that you really live in two separate worlds: Inner and Outer. You must focus on mastering the inner world more than the outer world.

Creating your dream life must happen from ***Inside-Out.*** Most of you are caught up in external circumstances to create the kind of life you want without realising that the *Outer World* can be changed by changing your *Inner World.*

The Outer World Is Only A Reflection Of What You Project In Your Inner World.

You can utilise the *Outer World* as a mirror to think deeply about the inner workings of your own mind. It is a potent method to look within yourself, to learn more about how you are actually creating your own life situations and circumstances that happen to you and in your physical reality, through the way you think and the way you feel.

The outer world is not as it appears to you; it is a reflection of your thoughts. Change your thoughts and feelings, and things in your outer world will change.

You can begin viewing life and yourself from a different perspective and the external world becomes more wonderful to you.

When the action of your inner world and outer world coincides, no power in the world can stop the externalisation of your desire but let it always spring from **"The Inner You ".**

Now when I coach someone, I help them to understand that there is no absolute world "out there", rather it is your own personalised world that you are constantly shaping as you go through life.

People, situations, and everything you experience are shaded by your perception of what is deep within your mind. You create and perceive the personalities of the people around you in your mind by using the building blocks of your thoughts.

You are lost in the external details to such an extent that you do not realise these details are only living pictures of what lies buried within your mind.

External events are the mirror of your deficiencies.

The cause of your displeasure lies not in the condition nor the person to whom you are displeased but, in the very self, you like so much. It is always your own blindness toward your real self that makes you dislike your own circumstances and situation in life. You surround yourself only with the true images of yourself only.

By choosing the path inwards, doing the *Inner Work*, and by being brave enough to rebuild your inner reality, you eventually rebuild your outer reality which is nothing else but a mirror of your *Inner World*!

As You Become Better, You Attract Better.

Your life is happening within you only and whatever you see in the outer world it exists inside your inner world.

The World Is a Mirror, Forever Reflecting What You Are Doing, Within Yourself.

- *Neville Goddard*

ACTIVITY - 1

This first activity is to critically observe yourself and this would reveal your current inner state through some deep self-realisation.

It is going to help you find the self that must be changed? And you will start the process of unlearning what is no longer serving you and finding new paths that are meant just for you.

Self- Analysis Questionnaire for Personal Inventory

1. In what areas of my life do I feel stuck? Where am I not getting the results, I want and how could it be better? What limiting belief or assumption is holding me back from growing?

2. Where in life do I feel that I have the strongest resistance to change? What fears related to it I am being called to confront. Which emotion do I feel frequently?

3. In which recent events I felt the need to hold back my emotions or I was judged for being vulnerable? When do I believe that this pattern originated?

4. What emotions and fears do I believe are hidden behind these patterns?

5. What emotions am I not allowing myself to feel and express?

6. Which limiting beliefs and assumptions are holding me back from adopting more supportive and life - enhancing habits? Am I overthinking?

7. Which present situation or event that I have the opportunity to see differently?

8. What related patterns are coming to light in my life?

9. Where in my life could I cultivate more joy?

10. What are the things that when I think about them, it brings me joy?

Having read and assimilated the information conveyed through this chapter, you are now ready to change what you do not like. You really do, you have the ability and nobody else can ever do it for you.

The Power Is Within You.

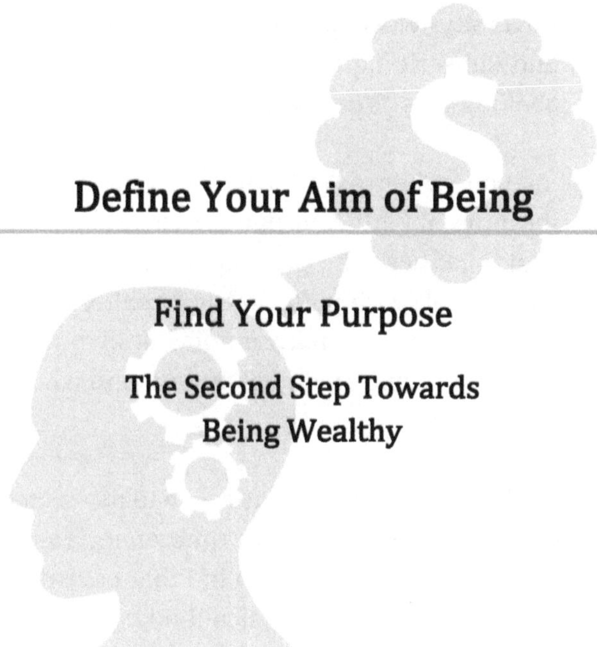

Define Your Aim of Being

Find Your Purpose

The Second Step Towards Being Wealthy

QUIT THE RATE RACE

All of you, for centuries, have been preoccupied with the traditional idea and thought of getting good grades, going to school, college, and university, working hard, saving, building assets, and subscribing to the perfect mediocre life, also labelling it as ***"The Good Life".***

Most of you, when asked who you are, normally identify yourself with your name, caste, religion, educational qualification, profession, etc. You only identify yourself with your physical reality and the outside world. You are unaware of your own reality, your true potential. You do not understand who you are at your core.

You have been taught your entire life to focus on the *Outer World* and to invest your time, energy, and effort in doing things to create a life that is visible to the naked eye like your physical body, plants, animals, etc. But you do not understand that there is an invisible world that creates the physical world. You do not understand the subject of life.

Most of us die without knowing the very fabric of our physical experience, who we are, and where our source is. What is the purpose of our life and how can we live the life of our dreams?

What This Means to You have gone to school, college and many educational institutions but no one has taught you the reality of your life. No one has taught you that the very fabric of your physical experience is space which is nothing but energy in nature. No one has taught you to invest in yourself before anyone else does.

Infinite Potential Lies in Your Being.

To invest in your inner self, knowing your Inner world, exploring the various different layers of your inner existence. Your inner being who holds the blueprint and knows the path of your ultimate destiny, who is aware of the fact that you are the ultimate profit-generating machine and infinite source of wealth creation, who is aware that you are the vortex of energy at your own core?

You are not taught that you can collapse the timeline between where you are and where you want to be which can increase your sense of happiness and aliveness in the present moment many-fold. And by clearing your old energetic blocks and limitations you can manifest your desires with ease and grace.

You Are a Multidimensional Human Being, Change-Maker, Thinker, And Creator!

You are not aware that infinite wisdom, creativity, abundance, and power dwell within you only.

And the irony is that you believe only what you can see, touch and feel and you do not want to listen and believe anything beyond that. You confine yourself in this finite body becoming the product of your environment and conditioning.

But the thing is that there are no rules. No one is aware that the things that you call rules were just made up by people who came before you and were trying to figure stuff out just like you are. These rules and constraints that you have on you were created by your parents, their parents, and their parents, who at one point were just kids trying to figure it out too.

Now when I coach someone, I do not tell them to break the laws but I tell them not to feel constrained by cultural rules, traditions, and expectations. It is all made up, and you can live life on your own terms.

I ask them to go within, check with themselves, have a meaningful conversation with their higher self, ask the wise question, and receive the right answers, and direction. I ask them to tap into the state of their ideal being to know the next step.

I ask them to have the courage to empty themselves of thoughts, images, beliefs, labels, tendencies, behaviours,

concepts, contexts, details, struggles, fears, desires, memories, personal stories, and social conditioning to know their real self. I ask them to have the courage to just witness the evolution of the universe and *"SIMPLY BE".*

"Life can be much broader once you discover one simple fact: Everything around you that you call life was made up by people that were no smarter than you. And you can change it, you can influence it...once you learn that, you will never be the same again."

–Steve Jobs

HUMAN DOING V/S HUMAN BEING

Human Doing is Masculine Energy. Human Being is Feminine Energy. But The world focuses on and rewards *Human Doings.* And because of the *"I Did*

This" stamp on everything, the element of being human is trampled underfoot by the need to perform and to do. Everyone focused on doing more, doing their "Best Work", rather than being more and being their "Best Self".

A world of *Human Doings* driving for success, fame, and fortune. This over-expressed need for achievement stems from a sense of self-worth that is built on *What You Do, Rather Than Who You Are at Your Core*. You tend to channel your emotional energy into getting things done. The unseen danger here for people who fall into the category of *"Human Doings"* is that they concentrate too much on external praise and material rewards instead of their true feelings, needs, and desires.

As a result, being the average human, you spend your entire life doing so many things, trying to fight off others who are trying to climb the same corporate ladder and it continues for many of the generations to come. Without being unaware of the fact that health, wealth, love, and happiness are a way of being, a state of mind, not necessarily a thing that you do and aim to achieve.

When I Coach someone, I help them understand that it is not like doing things to be successful, to be happy, and wealthy. It is like you are being successful, wealthy and you are happy. It is a way of being, feminine energy and state of mind you operate from. It is like how you think, how you act, how you make your decisions, how you hold yourself, how you conduct your relations.

You have to be first to receive all the amazing things that you are striving towards to manifest in your life.

Let your TO-BE list govern your TO-DO list. Let your feminine energy direct your masculine energy. Reflect on your inner purpose in life, find what you are passionate about, and let that drive your to-do list. Think the thoughts of your being, emit the right frequency from the place of existence of your desire, and soon your vision will become your reality in life. Lean back, stop doing, and start really being, tapping into your feminine energy.

Know exactly what you want and you must have it in your life. The reason these things manifest in your life is because you are being successful, you are being happy. You are watching the physical reality in real-time transported and created by invisible energy vibrations. Manifestation through being in positive energy vibration is instant; doing it in physical mode consumes more time.

That is why Human Beings are more important than Human Doings. Embrace the feeling of your being that you must want to be other than what you are. It's about being first and then going through the action of unfolding that state of being.

This Is the Secret Key to Doing Less and Having More in Life.

If you try to Be without Doing, you are Living in a Fantasy. If you try to Do without Being, you are Living in Frustration. Only when you Become the Person who can Do it, will you live the life of your dreams, will you have the perfect work-life balance and HAVE IT ALL!

It is not only about action. It is about vibrational alignment too. It is about the divine union of FEMININE and MASCULINE with in.

You Can Call the World into Being by Being the Thing You Would Call.

ACTIVITY - 2

This second activity helps you to reflect upon what you want to be in your life in future. It will help you find your purpose and formulate your ***"Aim of Being"***.

Self- Analysis Questionnaire for Personal Inventory

1. What is that *one thing* I always want to have in life, at any cost?

2. What do I desire to be, to have, to create, and what am I willing to let go of to make space for it?

3. What chapter of your life am I leaving behind and what energies am I inviting in?

4. What areas of my life do I want to *transform* the most? How much *income* do I want to create?

5. What sparks my interest that I would like to learn more about and become better at? Do I feel restricted?

6. What am I passionate about that has a greater good bigger than myself? What action steps can I take to be more of what I love to do?

7. What would I like to build, and what is my aim of being?

8. What is my vision for the future of humanity, and what would my role in it be?

9. What is coming to fruition in my life that I can be grateful for?

10. Where have I improved and can celebrate my progress?

Remind yourself that you are much bigger than you think you are and there is so much more to know every day no matter how far you have come.

Set your intention To Be what you really want with your heart and soul. Make it clear that this is something you really want more than anything in life. Make sure it gives you joy and it's important to you.

Your being is much bigger and larger than what you think it is.

Shift Your Identity

Live Your Purpose

The Third Step Towards Being Wealthy

KNOW YOUR BEING

You might be wondering why you must care about knowing your ***Inner Being.*** What does it mean to you? Well, the quality of your life, the way you experience life, it all depends on your level of consciousness of your being.

It is your Inner Being, inside you that ultimately decides the Quality of Life that you are living. You do not have control over the external world but if your inner self is calm, serene, and healthy then no matter what happens in the outer world, you will be free from its effect.

You would no longer be a football of the external situations or happenings of life. And if you get to this state of being healthy from the inside, then you are truly liberated from the bondage that this world offers.

And therefore, no one to change, no one to make whole, no one to purify - but self. It is a must for you to keep these states of your inner being healthy and ensure not to gather unwanted stuff any further.

You must gain a little deeper understanding of your being to distinguish between your individual identity and the shape it occupies to bring about a great transformation in your life.

Your Individual Identity Is Your Imagination, Your Definite Aim, Your Ideal Being Who You Want to Be.

You are free to choose the state you wish to identify yourself in, you can change your reality by changing you're feeling about yourself.

You might have taken a good look at your physical self but you are unaware of the existence of your Inner Self that has no face, form, or figure but it does mould itself into the structure by all that it consents to, by all that it believes. By understanding the deeper level of your existence, you must discover your true self to shift your identity.

You must be ever careful of where you are within yourself.

7 STATES OF CONSCIOUSNESS

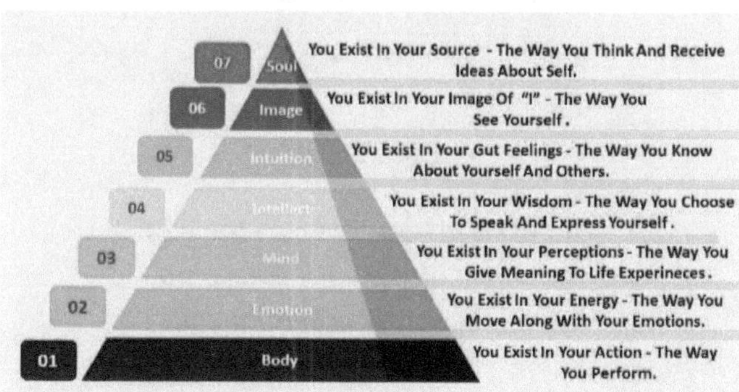

BODY

You exist in your actions, the way you perform.

Your physical body is what that soul takes to carry out its plan. It is really worth learning to listen to your body, rather than turning off its alarm signals time and again, ignoring them. Listen to the whispers of your body, so you will not have to hear the screams. Being totally present in your body is the road to freedom, to be free.

What This Means to You is that when you invest your time to learn, to listen and to understand your body, and your habitual actions, you align your actions, physical energy with your future aim of being.

You must be ever careful and aware of your actions to be in sync with your aim of being.

EMOTION

You exist in your energy, the way you move along with your emotions, the motives behind your actions.

Emotions are nothing but the energy that moves you. It shapes your choices, your action and ultimately your lives.

"Emotions" always start as "feelings". The feeling comes and goes without being or getting stuck. Feelings flow, like water in a river. The water of the feelings has turned into the ice of the emotion.

A feeling that is trapped, that got caught and crystallised in your being, connected to a certain event that was experienced in the past.

In that way, your emotion contains a charge, a heaviness, which holds it fixed in your being and which is aroused time and again when your system thinks it seems like a similar event occurring like the one which resulted in the crystallisation of feeling and emotion.

For instance, when you feel certain emotions that are angry or stressed, happy or peaceful you are not conscious of the energies stored in the body.

What This Means to You is that when you invest your time to be aware of your own emotions, your energies, these crystalized feelings in your body from past experiences and you learn how to better utilise this stored energy in a constructive way that aligns your emotional energy with your future aim of being.

You must be ever careful and aware of your actions, emotions to be in sync with your aim of being.

MIND

You exist in your perceptions the way you give meaning to life experiences.

The mind is the third state after the body and emotions. Your mind is the surface of your personality. This is the state of your being related to connection, connecting with yourself and connecting with everything and everyone with whom you enter into contact.

It is the faculty that helps you to perceive (see, hear, taste, smell, touch, and feel).

It is the contact point between you and the rest of the creation. Mind is the management of all actions. It is like an ocean where there are waves of thought energy you are creating every moment with your environment, with people, and with things around you. You cannot see it through your naked eye.

What This Means to You is that when you invest your time to improve your perception, you align your mental energy and thought to be in sync with your future aim of being.

You must be ever careful and aware of your actions, emotions and perceptions to be in sync with your aim of being.

INTELLECT

You exist in your wisdom, the way
you choose to speak and express
yourself - to you and others.

Intellect is the next state to the mind which actually has the ability to choose from the input the mind has just gotten from the outside environment through the five senses. *This state helps you to choose, to decide, and to discriminate whether something you hear is nice or not; whether something you taste is to your liking or not.*

The inner dialogue that always goes on (like "I do not like this, I do not agree" or "I like this, I agree", etc) is nothing but the intellect which is discriminating or judging everything.

What This Means to You is that when you invest your time to develop higher perspective and purify your power of true discrimination you align your wisdom to be in sync with your future aim of being.

You must be ever careful and aware of your actions, emotions, perceptions and wisdom to be in sync with your aim of being.

INTUITION

You exist in your gut feelings, the way you know about yourself and others.

Intuition is a very subtle state of your existence and plays a very crucial role in how intellect will work and what will be the condition of the mind. Intuition is more powerful than mind or intellect as it channels your feelings.

Intuition is a sixth sense, a "knowingness" which does not come to you from the rational mind or from the 5 senses — it comes from your higher self, your super conscious memory.

It is the faculty that helps you remember, and memorise all that you perceive through your mind (5 senses) and understand through your intellect.

In your present state, you experience memories from the past as patterns of behaviour. You habitually take on particular roles from these patterns, in response to situations with people. You react quite automatically and thoughtlessly, exactly like you did in the past.

These patterns of behaviour from the past experiences are triggered by how you feel in the present moment.

What This Means to You is that when you invest your time to be in touch with your intuition in the present moment you align your feelings to be in sync with your future aim of being.

You must be ever careful and aware of your actions, emotions, perceptions, wisdom and feelings to be in sync with your aim of being.

IMAGE

You exist in your self-image, your
"I", the way you see yourself.

"I am intelligent", "I am stupid", "I am rich", "I like this", basically the feeling of "**I-ness**" which is created when the soul identifies with the body.

The image of "I" represents the soul in a physical form. and it is the image of "I" that desires infest the heart.

The different shapes and manifestations of "I" separates you from everything else. You perceive yourself differently only on the basis of your self-image and Identity.

Your Identity Dictates Your Activities.

Changing the image of "I" results in a change in your habitual reaction, and a change of reactions results in a change in your world.

You are your centre of power, to act according to what you wish to represent in your life, for what you truly stand for in your life.

What This Means to You is that when you invest your time to discover your "I", what you want to represent in your life; you are aligning your image to be in sync with your future aim of being.

You must be ever careful and aware of your actions, emotions, perceptions, wisdom, feelings and image of "I" to be in sync with your aim of being.

SOUL

You exist in your source - the way you think and receive ideas about self.

The soul is the subtlest state of your existence and consciousness. Sitting in the innermost layer the soul witnesses and is aware of everything that happens in all the other different layers of your inner existence.

In the process of entering the physical body, the consciousness sleep itself into thinking that it has become a body made of solid matter.

"To awaken your consciousness, you must identify yourself with your being, the soul itself."

The purpose of every soul is to get liberated, whether you know or do not know, whether you accept or do not accept.

You are a seeker seeking the truth and the truth is your soul only.

What This Means to You is that when you invest your time to release this identification of "I" you can find out what and what you really are: not the body or personality, but infinite spirit, you align your source to be in sync with your future aim of being.

You must be ever careful and aware of your actions, emotions, perceptions, wisdom, feelings, image of "I" and source to be in sync with your aim of being.

THE SUPER CONSCIOUSNESS

Having discovered that everything in your world is a state of consciousness made visible, you must clearly define the particular state that you want to be visible. By Defining your aim, you are defining a state of consciousness - which, like all states of consciousness, must have its reactions to life.

Your aim of being must be clearly defined, "what do you want?"

You can easily tell whether you are faithful to your aim, your ideal being, and what you want to be in life by watching your reactions to daily events.

Your reactions are only a state of consciousness that attracts the situations and circumstances of your life. You can easily separate yourself from all the reactions, and moods which you have taken as normal and are identified with them if you see them as your inner state not as outer situations and circumstances.

Being in alignment with your ideal being with all the different states of your identity can bring profound bliss, abundance, peace and joy in your life.

What This Means to You is that your life experiences consist of your state of consciousness in these four states of your Inner Identity *(Mind, Intellect, Intuition & Image).*

Whatever experiences you are going through are the permutation and combination of your awareness in these four states of your inner identity. Your purpose is to go from one level to another level to live in a higher level of identity and consciousness to become financially free.

This internalisation of consciousness allows you to take joy inside.

You realise that the pleasure you feel in enjoying the world is really primarily in the heart.

ACTIVITY - 3

This third activity helps you to notice your reaction and habitual behaviour in regards to your aim of being.

Assume the identity of your ideal being, the person you want to be and ***Observe Your Daily Reaction on All Levels of Your Being Physically, Emotionally, Mentally, Psychologically, Financially, Socially and Spiritually.***

Self- Analysis Questionnaire for Personal Inventory

1. Where do I feel, in which state of inner existence I am still holding myself back from being fully me, due to fear of others' judgement or backlash?

2. What are my limiting beliefs and assumptions that are preventing me from being so?

3. Am I experiencing low energy, negative thoughts and emotions frequently? Do I find it difficult to go with flow?

4. Do I find it difficult to focus and have no will power? Do I resist change?

5. What are the results (people, circumstances and situation) that are created and manifested in life? Am I not getting the desired results?

6. Do I react or respond if a disappointing situation occurs?

7. Do I find it difficult to identify my aim of being? Do I have clarity?

8. Do I find it difficult to express myself in an effective way? Do I practise conscious silence?

9. Do I seek validation and constant approvals? Do I lack confidence, authority and assertiveness?

10. Where do I feel, in which state of existence, is my conditioning holding me back the most?

You cannot be different from what you are now unless you begin to separate yourself from your present reaction and to identify yourself with your aim of being.

Use the power of your body, your energy, your mind, your will, your heart, your atmosphere, your being alive, here and now. This may be hard at the beginning, but it will become your natural state of being very soon.

You must practise detaching yourself from your negative moods and thought patterns.

Create Your New Reality

Build Your Purpose

The Fourth Step Towards Being Wealthy

5 ELEMENTAL STAGES OF CREATION

"I am not my body, Nor my mind!"
"I am a play of five elements; a state of consciousness; a drama of spirit dancing with Joy and Sorrow".

-Kabir

These 5 "elements" – space, air, water, fire and earth – very clearly show the elemental stages of creation. Each of the elements represents a state of matter. Earth is all solid, water is all liquid, the air is all movement, fire is all transformation and that transforms one form of matter into the other and that keeps all matter together is space or ether. This is how they manifest in nature.

These elements also describe the stages of the soul's (spirit) descent into matter, and, when reversed, the progressive stages of its liberation.

They also represent stages of manifestation outward from spirit to matter. Where *Space* is the energy out of which the first atoms *(Idea)* were born, *Air* as representing the gases *(Movement of Thoughts)* like attracts like, *Fire* the stars *(Will-power)* gives the initial shape-transformation,

Water (Melted State of Matter) as it cools still further and *Earth* as *(Matter)* that has cooled sufficiently to become a solid physical manifestation.

You are the product of the same process of creation. you are infinite energy that has been converted into a fixed form you call yourself; you have the power to change this form. all your immediate experiences, attitudes, opinions, beliefs and character, are composed of these 5 elements of creation only.

If asked to change your character, you will say it is not possible. Your character is a form that is fixed. But it is only a form of the infinite energy that has been locked into a fixed physiological form. You may feel even your mental opinions cannot be changed. Each of your opinions is a form of energy, and if you know how the opinion has been formed, you can change it.

You can change your attitude, behaviour, your character and identity. Character is the form; life experiences bring forces to influence that form and give it shape or expression. This formless Inner Self, the so-called "I" which is then projected as your environment and conditions of life.

You must disentangle the "I"
from these fixed ideas, forms,
shapes, and manifestations with
which you have lived for so
many years.

Everything follows the same rule where that infinite energy is being moulded into these different forms. The only thing that makes a difference is your awareness and level of consciousness of this process of creation.

These five subtle elements are the essence of the creation of the entire world both within you and outside. They form the basis for all things found in material creation, from a grain of sand to the complex physiology of every human being.

You are a dance of mass. Let me help you to retrace your consciousness from matter to spirit, to reverse the route by which you first came into physical form. Follow the definite stages of awakening in your awareness of who and what you really are.

SPACE

The Space element is the most powerful and dominant. It represents expansion, potential, possibilities, and enhancement. It governs your structure and execution. For everything to exist, it needs space. Space has no form, no shape, it cannot be touched or seen.

This element is infinite, boundless, calming, and soothing. Enhancing the space element helps you smoothly sync your source energy with the universal energies. To strengthen the space element, surround yourself with the colour blue.

If there is no space nothing can exist. regularly clean your mental, emotional, physical, and social space to receive pure positive source energy.

Let the best idea enter your space
to convert into physical reality.

AIR

The Air element represents growth and is associated with movement and change. Air is your most basic connection to life as it heightens your sense of relationship with life in its countless forms and shapes of *physical manifestation based on the prolonged existence of the idea in your space.*

Like Attracts Like.

In a balanced state air element activates inspiration and creativity. To strengthen the air element, resolve to wake up early to allow ample time for all the things that need to get done before the work day commences.

Invest time watching clouds float around in the sky. Get outdoors for a morning walk, and fill your lungs, eyes, and ears with the clarity and peace that this time offers.

Your body can only survive if you breathe.

FIRE

The Fire element brings transformation. It is the will power, the driving force behind all life forces. The sun represents this element. Though fire is one of the strongest elements, it is the hardest to balance. It is very important to connect with the fire element and keep it balanced.

Fire represents the inner guiding light that helps destroy all doubts and negative thoughts. Regulating your inner fire is essential for moving ahead in life with zest.

Fire element inspires you to take continuous inspired action in the direction of the idea which has existed in your mind for a long time now.

Fire has to do with your tact, passion, and generosity, as well as managing your emotions. Though fire in its positive form is transformation, it can also result in negative traits like rage, hatred, greed, envy, and the desire for revenge. It is a very dynamic element, a quality that can become overly aggressive if it is not properly tempered. Too much fire can be explosive, and too little can make you "cold".

To strengthen the fire element, the early morning sun can heal many diseases and depression. Go on a brisk walk and thank you sun for providing you the energy to run through the day.

WATER

The water element is adaptive and it is a huge life force. It has to nurture and protect energies as it influences your ability to go with the flow of emotions - and your inner wisdom or ability to "reflect" on things and find clarity.

It is the molten state of the physical manifestation of the idea and it represents flow. go with the flow while attaching yourself to your idea.

To strengthen the water element, drink loads of water throughout the day, and keep your energies moving and flowing.

Acknowledge and respect all your feelings without labelling them as good or bad, positive or negative. Express as much as you can. Try and share your feelings with anyone you feel close to or you can trust.

Practice swimming as it is a great activity to soothe and heal the body and mind. It pulls out negativity, feelings, and intuition and makes your mind calm and focused.

EARTH

The Earth element is inert, unmoving, and the most powerful of all elements. It represents reliability, and stability like a tree deeply rooted in the soil that will sway in the wind but not fall over. It is your basis and grounding. When you Invest in the earth's element of solidity, it enhances the strength of your mind, determination, uninterrupted advancement, and attachment toward your goal.

It represents the solidity of your idea in physical form.

To strengthen the earth's elements, stay in touch with the physical experience of walking, standing, or sitting on the ground sometime during the day. Be grounded while keeping your head high. Always remember to attach yourself to your aim of being in sync with your source and let the flow of energy happen from upward to downward and then from downward to upward again.

What This Means to You *is you invest* some time to understand these elements and relate to them. Your physical form, shape, and expression represent the *Earth Element,* your feeling, emotion, and flow represent the *Water Element,* your heat, control, willpower and transformation represent the *Fire Element,* your thought, sensation, and vibration represent the *Air Element,* and your pure awareness, consciousness, and infinite potential is your *Space Element.*

Once you understand five elements of creation and the process of creation you are empowered to let your thoughts, ideas convert into your reality. You realise the source of creative energy within you only.

You Start To "Do Less & Relax More".

THE VORTEX FULL OF SOURCE ENERGY

"You are an energy field, operating in a larger energy field."

–James Ray

You are a creation of eternal energy going through a journey in different forms. You are energy living in this body, having a marvellous mind. You are an observer, a witness, something which is permanent.

You are spirit in the flesh. Therefore, the pure essence of you has always been and always will be. You are a pure energy extension of one universal energy. You are a spiritually energetic being!

Everything in the universe is energy. This energy can never be created or destroyed. It is moving into the form, through form, and out of form. It just changes form.

This universal energy knows everything about you, your past, present, and future. It knows the very purpose of your life, your talents, and the unique qualities you have, it knows all your likes and dislikes. It has solutions to all your problems. It has the power to attract desired people and situations in your life. It has the power to make your dreams/ desires come true. It holds everything you could ever want and imagine.

Deep at the centre of your being, your heart, your soul there is a vortex of source energy that is nothing but pure positive love, an infinite well of love.

Allow this love to flow to the surface, to fill your heart, your mind, your consciousness, your very being, and radiates out from you in all directions.

The more love you give, the more you have to give, the supply is endless. Love is an expression of inner joy, use it to make you feel good. Love is the highest frequency you can vibrate on.

What This Means to You is that whatever you do in life, always watch your heart. Watch your feelings. You will notice that there is a ray of energy, of force, going out from your heart toward people, things, or expectations.

You must learn to control and redirect that energy. The more you direct this upward towards universal energy, the more you will find your every desire is being fulfilled, always in the best possible way.

This is most powerful when you are in alignment with your Higher Self in the vortex, you simply by thinking of a goal, or a wish, can create the equivalent manifestation of that goal in the vortex of universal energy. You will find all things always work out for you.

This makes you one with the universal mind and you use this resource of creative energy, to create the life of your dreams. Make your higher self your companion on the path.

This attitude draws more grace into your life because there is less of the thought of "I" in it, and more of the thought of allowing source energy and love to flow through you. Consciously connecting with this vortex, source energy is the key to a happy, prosperous, and purposeful life.

Whatever you think and feel at any point in time determines your frequency. You have an aura, your energy field, that is not visible to the naked eye, but it creates your own power of attraction.

Your personal energy is the most powerful currency on the planet.

The key elements that influence your personal energy are your thoughts, feelings, emotions, values, beliefs, and actions. Your personal energy determines the quality of your life. The more the alignment and presence of the universal energy in your personal space, the better the quality of your actions, results, and thus life.

You vibrate at a certain frequency and vibrate at a higher frequency; you can have all the resources you need to be financially free and to be extraordinarily wealthy and successful. Vibrating on a lower frequency can bring you out of alignment, away from your vortex, your source energy which makes you experience resistance, distractions, problems, and pains.

The world moves around you based on the frequency you are vibrating on; you do not need to move at all. You are always at your centre whatever the reality is.

What This Means to You is that if you are witnessing the pictures that have appeared are not what you want, learn to let go of the thoughts of limitation, and old beliefs and think new thoughts of what you want to create, feel them, and be grateful in advance that it is done and your wish is being created in reality.

If you are experiencing a lack it is because you are looking at the outside world and people as supply. It is not people who are giving you things you desire.

They can be one channel through which the universe is answering your every command. But the channels and the supply both are unlimited.

When you receive anything, remember that you attracted it to you by the law of attraction, by being on the frequency of love and in harmony with the universal supply.

Non acceptance and creating resistance inside, disconnect you from the source, leading to wrong actions and wrong results in life. Learn the unconventional inner path of non - resistance to live a happy and fulfilled life.

For a strong connection with your source energy, your soul, you must choose to vibrate at a higher frequency in alignment with your aim of being and make the best use of the different inner states of your being (thoughts, feelings, words, and perception).

You must be aware of your personal energy in all states of your being to be in alignment with your soul, your aim of being.

You must internalise your level of consciousness, your worldview, your observation, and your expression to be in alignment with source energy, your soul.

You must take positive action to love and accept yourself first and to align yourself with this higher frequency of love and your aim of being. To be the best version of you that feels good, that is passionate, that is enjoying life — that is aligned with your truth.

If you are feeling good you are aligned to source and soul then you are aligned to your potential. That is, you being happy at the moment which is a powerful creative energy to be in.

Now when I coach someone, I help them learn the two most important Life Skills, one is mastery over one's focus (concentration) on desired aim of being, and the other one is mastery over one's emotions (energy) to strengthen their connection with source energy in order to raise their vibration.

Once you raise your vibrations and your level of consciousness you must find your hidden talents, the unique purpose for which you are born to live a wealthy life. Once you start living, building, and serving your natural inborn purposes, your aim of being, your actions are automatically focused, perfect, and responsible to manifest your desire into reality.

True wealth is not only your job, your salary, your bank account, your investments, your spouse, or your parents. Your true wealth is your ability to vibrate at the highest frequency of love for yourself and others and to connect with the cosmic power that creates all things.

Learn to live in a constant state of alignment and connection with your soul, your creative source of energy to create your own reality. You are a creation of eternal creative energy and the power of creation is within you only.

You Are the Ultimate Profit Generating Machine And The Source Of Wealth Is Within You Only.

ACTIVITY - 4

This fourth activity helps you to attach and align your energies to your desired aim of being.

Accept the idea of your being on all levels of your energetic existence. Vibrate on a higher frequency of love and gratitude to create your desire into reality.

Self- Analysis Questionnaire for Personal Inventory

1. What limiting beliefs do I feel ready to release? What assumptions am I willing to detach from?

2. What old ways of thinking, feeling, living and behaving am I ready to release and let go of?

3. Do I vibrate on a higher frequency of love, joy and peace?

4. Do I frequently see and notice the evidence of my desire, in your environment?

5. Am I being in flow with life having the image in my mind in alignment with what I desired to create in my life? What meanings do I give to my life experiences?

6. Do I visualise it quite often, my ideal being in full picture, on all levels of my existence.

7. Do I see myself already there what I want to be? What do I think about myself?

8. What would I say? How would I say it? How will I present myself?

9. How do I feel about myself? What do I have to offer? How Do I channel my emotions?

10. Do I have that picture, Images, vision of my future self and do I see it every now and then?

11. What actions Am I inspired to take? Where do these actions lead me, to what results?

Keep your focus on your ideal being and attach all your energy to the presence of your ideal being. Look for the evidence around and accept the idea of your ideal being on all elemental stages of creation.

Start speaking your intention,
your desire to be extraordinarily
wealthy, successful and vibrate on
a higher frequency of love for
wealth and abundance.

Unlock Your Wealth Potential

Serve Your Purpose

The Final Step Towards Being Wealthy

THE MOST VALUABLE ASSET

Are you trying to accumulate wealth by striving, slaving, or working hard? You do not need to do that. The effortless way is the best way to create wealth in your life.

You are the most valuable and infinite asset of your life portfolio. You are the ultimate source of wealth and the only asset that matters is you.

Realising your true self, when you begin to invest in yourself you become a physical and financial asset that can be developed, reinvested, and most importantly, if things go wrong with your physical wealth, you are able to start over with the knowledge and experience you have trained yourself in.

You are the most valuable asset where you must put your time, energy, and money, and yet you are probably the one thing that tends to get neglected in life. When other people's priorities come up or it is time to sacrifice something you might be the first to bend.

As humans, this is what you have been told your whole life. You are constantly told what to do, how to act, and who to be. With so many external influences, pursuing the life you want and staying true to yourself can be challenging.

Investing in yourself, and in your dreams is not a selfish act. You must choose to invest in yourself in a way that brings you closer to your goals, your aim of being which aligns with your aspiration and purpose in life.

When you know exactly what would make you feel fulfilled, it becomes much easier to figure out what kind of investments you need to make in yourself to get there.

And as long as you are making investments that align with your aim of being, there is no such thing as wasted effort.

What This Means to You is that true wealth extends to your money's ability to work for yourself, to your ability to embrace the skills and uniqueness you possess, your ability to maintain healthy, happy, professional, and personal relationships, and your ability to love and accept yourself fully.

It relies heavily on your emotional intelligence and you become adaptable to outside circumstances. It extends to your ability to serve your higher purpose, aligning yourself with higher frequencies of health, wealth, love, and happiness.

Wealth Is Your Ability to Fully Experience Life.

CREATE SUSTAINABLE WEALTH

You may think that wealth is how much money, bank balance you have, physical assets or properties you own, right? You may think being rich means more money in the bank A/C or other investments but all for sure in monetary terms.

These may be conventional ideas of wealth but those who have acquired this monetary wealth know that true wealth goes beyond your physical and material wealth.

Infinite thoughts and ideas in your mind are equal to cash in your pocket in countless ways. Your true source of wealth consists of the ideas in your mind, you give your acceptance to.

Your thoughts result in the acquisition of knowledge. Instil the right thought that aligns with your aim of being, the one you would like to be.

Direct your thoughts towards what you do want rather than what you do not want. Your goals must prioritise the things you care about most. This will keep your creative energy flowing in the direction of your goals and dreams.

"Wherever our attention goes, energy flows."

Every individual is rich and wealthy in that particular subject of life wherever they have decided to give their attention and focus to. You are wealthy in direct proportion to your energy, the acceptance that you have given to any idea and thought in your mind.

What This Means to You is that when you build into your mentality the acceptance for the idea of "Wealth", you create sustainable wealth. *Let the idea of wealth consume your mind - your mental energy.* Let your mind accept and acquire the state of your desired aim of being. Look for evidence of abundance and give it to your mind.

Your dominant idea or belief, what you really feel to be true does not produce a mental conflict or argument. It is all possible if you believe that what you are seeking and giving acceptance to is possible to obtain.

The feeling of wealth produces Wealth. It gradually awakens your love for wealth and makes you vibrate powerfully on the higher frequency of love, prosperity, and abundance. Fall in love and *let the love for wealth consume your heart - your emotional energy.* If you feel abundant internally, it will become so externally.

Be wealthy in your spirit and take action from the place of abundance. Assume that you are already wealthy and focus on finding the evidence and the presence of abundance and wealth in your environment.

Do the thing you love to do, and do it for the joy and thrill of it. Let your heart take charge of your body. *Let your dream drive you to take joyful, inspired action to consume - your physical energy.* You must separate yourself from your present reactions to life and attach them to your aim in life.

Fall in love with your ideal being, that ideal state to the point it haunts the mind, moved enough from your present reactions, attach them to your aim in life and you would externalise that desired state of being within your world.

Now when I coach someone, I help them understand that wealth is a sub-conscious conviction. A little transformation in mood is not the real transformation. It requires you to remain in that assumed state of wealth and abundance for long enough to make it stable so that all your energies are flowing from this desired aim of being. Even if what you are assuming that you are at the moment denies it, your reason denies it. But you no longer think of that state. You are thinking from that state of wish being fulfilled.

Having moved from one state into the other, you have altered your relationship relative to the world around you, and that changed relationship compels a change in behaviour relative to the world. So, people have to act differently towards you.

What This Means to You is that it all starts with you defining your aim of being, your desire to be financially free, wealthy and successful.

Desire is the spring of all action,
for you must want to be other
than what you are, what you
want to be.

ACTIVITY - 5

This final activity helps you to externalise your assumed identity, your ideal being - into your physical reality by assuming the filling of your wish is fulfilled. It helps you to Master yourself - your thoughts, feelings and actions.

Self- Analysis Questionnaire for Personal Inventory

1. To what thoughts am I consuming? What am I saying to myself and others?

2. Am I disciplined to think only the state I desire, my aim of being to realise, denying the evidence of the senses?

3. With what feeling am I identified?

4. Am I disciplined to imagine and entertain only those feelings that contribute to my aim?

5. With what actions am I consenting?

6. Am I disciplined to act on that conviction of the wish fulfilled?

7. Am I able to control my thoughts, feelings and actions? Yes Or No

Never think wrong in any shape or form, nor entertain an undesirable feeling. You must act and move away from negative thoughts and feelings. Do not dwell on the imperfection of yourself or others, it impresses limitations within you. Self-control is your highest achievement.

A Change of Impression Results in A Change of Expression. A Change of Feeling Is the Change of Pattern.

- Neville Goddard

PART THREE

THE UNCONVENTIONAL WAY TO WEALTH

PROSPERITY WITH PEACE

Trinity Of Wealth - Within

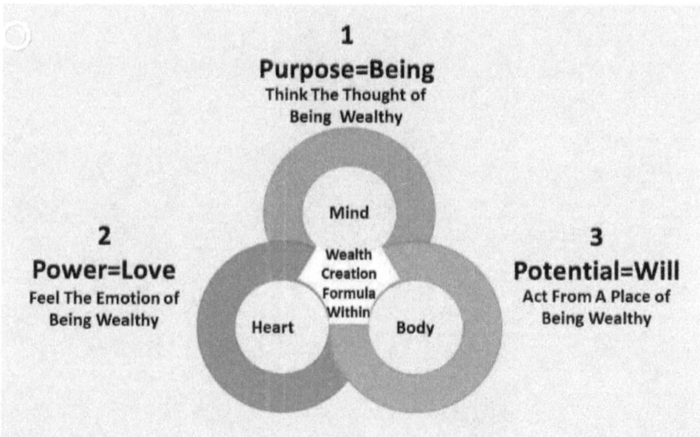

YOUR PURPOSE IS YOUR "BEING"

"Think The Thought of Being Wealthy"

Your life is what your thoughts are in your mind. Thoughts that you think in your mind every second of every minute of every hour of the day. Thoughts are nothing but energy having frequencies and vibrations. Train yourself to think the thoughts that make you feel wealthy. This way you will always be creating your life out of wealth and wealth always brings more to be wealthy about.

Everything that has ever been created first existed as a thought. The beauty of thoughts is, they do not just determine your internal world; they can determine your external world as well. Thoughts keep whispering in your head and make you feel good or bad. Put your awareness into practice. Find a more optimistic thought and focus on things of well-being and wealth.

You can be anything in this world you desire to be, if you clearly define your aim in life and constantly occupy that aim of being. It must be habitual. The concept is the thought, an idea that you hold of yourself you must put on not just for a moment and you are not going to return to your restrictions, old images that were prior in your mind.

"The Power of Attention, Your Concentrated Energy"

The different possibilities and outcomes depend only on one thing, where and what you are focusing upon? The moment you focus on something, that object begins to move toward you. Sounds like a magnet? You are indeed a powerful magnet. You attract people, stuff, and events using the enormous mental energy of your thoughts. It is all possible if you believe that what you are seeking is possible to obtain. If you build the right and powerful thoughts and ideas into your mind, using the law of focus in the right manner you can achieve everything you want in your life.

The more you dwell on what you do not want, the more of it you create. Your strong desire may be that you do not want lack and scarcity, but since you are focusing on them repeatedly, you are giving them energy and thus they grow.

Concentrated observation of one thing shuts out other things and causes them to disappear. Your Attention is a form of energy.

When you think or speak about lack, you are giving it the energy of your attention. This causes it to manifest in physical reality. What you put your attention on grows and becomes permanent in your life.

It could be wealth. It could be a success. It could be an object of your desire or something abstract like courage or violence. It could be something positive or negative. It could be something you want or do not want. That does not matter, whatever it is, it will grow if you give it the energy of your attention. That is why, you must formulate an aim and constantly notice yourself in regard to that aim.

You formulate an aim to see yourself right into the situations of that desired end. You start thinking from your end instead of just thinking of your desired end. You learn the art of thinking from the end result that you want.

Your only job is to learn to think from that end - even if your reason denies it, your senses deny it, though everything in your environment and surrounding denies it. You occupy that end.

You must Start thinking from your aim of being. And focus on having wealth and abundance. Focus on faith, happiness, and success. Focus on what you want and do things that make you feel good.

Be with people who make you feel good. Eat things that make your body feel good. Go to a place that makes you feel good. Find out the evidence of wealth and abundance. Read it, talk about it, and spread the message. Eventually, you will start experiencing the evidence of it in your physical reality.

The good news is: There is no right time to start, you can choose your aim of being what you want to be at this very moment while reading this book.

You can start now, from scratch, you do not need to raise large capital, and you do not need to have a single penny in advance if you only invest the next moment, the next thought wisely.

Your Thought Is Your Gold Coin That God Has Given to You and By Using It Wisely You Can Turn Your Broken Year into Net Profit.

The moment you understand and learn the law of thought to use it in your favour, you are empowered to create wealth and abundance in your life.

When a thought arises in your mind, it is reflected in your voice, strengthened by your feeling and emotion, and the laws of thought will manifest in your life.

There is nothing in this world that can be drawn into your world unless you - and you alone call him. For what you seek is seeking you.

"Seek wealth and wealth will seek you back."

-Reetu Goyal Kansal

YOUR POWER IS "YOUR LOVE"

"Feel The Emotion of Being Wealthy"

Your feelings are vital in achieving your dream and accomplishing anything that you set out to do. Feelings and emotions are what give force and power to your thoughts.

Your feelings are like your extended sense, your intuition, that goes beyond merely the physical and allows you to see in an intuitive way, your way to life around you. You have to literally feel your way to wealth.

You are capable of controlling the way you think and feel about wealth if you use the language of wealth versus the vocabulary of lack. You can speak things into existence using the law of vibration.

The words you speak are indicative of thoughts and feelings. Your words are an immediate reflection of your feelings. Any wise person can determine what you are going to attract in your life just by listening to your words.

Remember to keep your words positive regarding your desired end result, and appreciate all positive words you can hear about your desires for wealth and abundance. Your words have the power to cleanse your mind of wrong ideas.

Be careful not to utter words that would work against your ability, any situation, or achieving your goal. Negative words and statements suck all the positive energy.

What This Means to You is that as you go about your day, listen to the words you say. If the words do not match the experience you describe, either you are not in touch with what is really going on or you are not in touch with your true feelings. Either one is a starting point and gives you a basis to realise you must work to know your feelings.

Let me warn you here that the biggest obstacle to working through feelings is not feeling emotions. As young children, you go through many experiences that are too much for you, you simply don't have the brains to process everything that you eventually have as an adult.

Learning the rules is a painful process, which results in a lot of suppression of feelings.

During your upbringing, you are taught to learn to deal with other people and society. Instead of learning to listen to your feelings, you learn to suppress your feelings. As a result, you use tricks, which cause you not to feel all kinds of feelings anymore.

By blocking out your feelings and not allowing yourself to actually feel the way that you do, when you feel it, you are doing a great disservice to yourself. By cutting off completely a part of who you are, and not paying attention to what is going on inside of you emotionally, you lose one of your greatest senses, and vital tools for seeing and using to navigate your way to the world around you.

Now when I coach someone, I help them to learn to listen to their feelings and to be able to interpret and understand the messages that they bring to them. I help them to be vulnerable as it is nothing else than (daring to) say what you feel, what hurts you, that you experience pain when someone else says or does this or that, what you find unpleasant in your life. As a result, they are more aware of their own self and how they feel about it.

Your Feeling Is What Counts.

Ask yourself what do you feel about your life when it comes to wealth? What are your beliefs around and about wealth? *Your Feelings are the secret path. Only an emotional move holds the power to create your desired result.*

The feeling of wealth produces wealth. You must deliberately wear the feelings of wealth, acknowledge the thoughts of wealth you have, and use the powerful words that bring your desired result until it is all-natural.

The moment the feeling of being wealthy becomes natural it will begin to bear fruit within your world. Changing the feelings of your self-image, your "I" whom you are identified with will bring the desired result, a change in your reaction; that change of a reaction is a change in your environment and behaviour. Your reactions are automatic and so if your image of "I" and your feelings are changed it would automatically change your reaction to life.

Your Identity, Your Image Of "I",
Dictates Your Activity.

What This Means to You is that you think and feel the emotion of love for yourself and others as you are being wealthy and abundant. Love is the feeling with high energy and frequency that can dissolve all your past traumas, and mental sufferings, open all your emotional blocks, and make you flow freely in the ***"River of Life"*** being healthy, wealthy, happy, and abundant.

And when you successfully make the feelings, thoughts, and words of love for wealth, you will manifest the same in your physical experience and they influence your reality.

All these positive abundant feelings therefore soon have manifested in your physical world. Be hungry to really bring about the change in the self, change the feeling of "I".

When you feel abundant, you feel
fulfilled, you feel loved and not
poor, hatred, ill or mediocre.

- Reetu Goyal Kansal

YOUR POTENTIAL IS "YOUR WILL"

"Act From a Place of Being Wealthy"

The potential is your will, your urge to bring about the change. It depends if you are hungry enough to bring about the change in self as it all starts with your definite aim, your desired aim of being.

Having discovered the self, the one you would like to be other than what you are. You assume you are what you want to be. You choose to remain in that assumed and accepted state for long enough to make it so stable that all of your energies flow from the state of being wealthy. You are no longer thinking of that desired state. But you are thinking and acting from that state.

You just do what you would do if you knew you were wealthy. You act as if you have already received your desire. If you come and act from a place of emotional scarcity of feeling fear, anxiety, and lack, then you are sure to manifest such things in your life.

You must place trust in your actions and behave like you have that total ***conviction of being wealthy****. Anytime acting from a place of a lower vibrational* *emotion is bringing you down, can you recognize it, feel it, and transmute it to a more positive one?*

This Is the Foundation of Turning Your Thought into Reality or The Ability To "Transmute" Your Experience at Your Will.

It takes a degree of mental stamina and involves your mind, your higher perspectives, the way you give meaning to different experiences of life.

The seemingly opposite things are actually one and the same. The only difference is that they vibrate at varying degrees and different frequencies.

A simple example of this is hot and cold. Cold is just the absence of heat and heat is just the absence of cold. But they are both one thing: temperature, vibrating on different frequencies and at varying degrees.

Physical matter and spiritual energy are the same thing, with spiritual energy vibrating at a much higher level, such that it cannot be perceived by our senses. Love and hate are two ways of experiencing the same thing, a relationship towards something.

Similarly, being wealthy and mediocre are the two ways of experiencing the same thing, a relationship with self.

What This Means To You Is That takes the feeling of lack or scarcity, you feel for self: is there any way you can shift it to the feeling of being abundant, for example?

Every coin has two sides. The third side is that dimension that you choose to look at.

There is always a space between stimuli and response, where you choose to act as per your will. No matter what happens to you in your life, you alone have the capacity to choose your response, your action, and your reaction towards it. You must choose to separate yourself from your present reactions to life and attach them to your aim in life.

If you choose to focus and perceive the world from your dual eyes you experience lack and face the fear of scarcity.

If you choose to turn your focus within, perceive the world from your mind's eye, and see the clear vision, potential, and possibilities for your breakthrough to create wealth and abundance in your life which is your birthright.

What This Means to You is that you start entertaining the idea of being wealthy, accept that state in your mind that you are the wealthy one you want to be, and notice your reaction throughout the day in regard to your aim of being. Your reactions will tell you the state in which you are operating.

You must act from the place of your aim, practising inner separation, moving psychologically away from all the negative thoughts, moods and habitual reactions to different experiences of life that makes you feel less.

You cannot be different from what you are now unless you detach yourself from your negative reactions in the midst of all the troubles and disasters of daily life.

Separating yourself from your negative inner states of being, attaching yourself to the acceptance of your wish being fulfilled, and taking action from that place, will raise you to higher and higher levels of consciousness.

First, you must upgrade your thoughts, and your worldview, change the feeling of "I", your self-image, raise your vibration to a higher frequency, and take action from your assumed state of being while shifting your identity.

This will bring more wealth and abundance into your life. Always remember that it is your state of consciousness that attracts your life.

The state to which you consent must be made manifest in your life.

Invest Your Time Wisely

The Art of Investment

You are aware that you can turn your ideas into gold, and thoughts into reality. Now you build your understanding that your time is your real money and each moment is a gold coin in your pocket.

If you do not like what you are encountering in your daily life then learn the art of investing your time wisely.

Be more conscious of every moment of the day, not to spend it as "to waste", but you must invest it for a purpose, for which a profit is expected.

For everything in life, it must be a conscious investment. Every moment of time is an opportunity to invest, not to spend. Know that everything is before you, not far away from you, a state of wealth and abundance or a state of lack, scarcity or poverty.

So, if you invest every moment of time with a purpose, you not only hope but can expect a great reward, a profit on your investment.

What This Means to You is that every moment, you become conscious of that moment. What are you thinking? What are you feeling? What are you doing?

You accept yourself as a wealthy human being and you do not allow yourself to hear or accept anything as true other than that which contributes to the noble concept you hold of yourself, which is being abundant and having everything that you need.

Now when I coach someone, I help them to admit, to give their consent to, using the moment as the very moment to invest in their ideal being - even if their reason denies it, their sense denies it, their environment and outer circumstances denies it.

I ask them to use the 5 elemental states of creation and transmute their energy to proceed in that assumed state of being, knowing that it will take some time to take shape but I ask them to continue vibrating on a higher frequency of their wish being fulfilled.

Your inner conviction of your ideal being is the key to experiencing it in reality. This is called ***The Law***

Of Being. As long as this law is working you do not need any money to become wealthy if you only accept that you are already wealthy.

Whatever you are thinking, feeling, and doing now is not going to go away. It is going to move forward and get visible itself as a condition, as the circumstances of your life.

I understand at this moment, being wealthy and successful may seem distant and even unapproachable to you from what you think and feel of yourself to be. But the simple thought that you are not wealthy enough is what keeps you from being free! If you could break even this one idea, you would go into experiencing it.

Wealth and Success are not something you have to acquire, in truth, you have them already; you just have not fully realised it, you have not experienced it.

And you will keep living a pseudo-life until you accept the self that needs to be changed. You do everything to maintain a fake image, a false idea, under the influence of society, being conditioned all your life. And then a point comes in your life when this false image becomes your cage.

You cannot really become aware of that cage until you start investing in yourself and invest yourself wisely to train your mind to imagine and visualise yourself in that infinite state of wealth and abundance; identify yourself with it in order to awaken within you that lost memory of what you are in reality- children of infinity. For that alone is what you really are.

"You are the abundant child of the universe; abundance is your birthright!"

- Reetu Goyal Kansal

Congratulations!

I am so proud of you for making the great decision to explore your full potential and know what you do know to be extraordinarily wealthy and successful. I truly admire and respect you for wanting to be wealthy and successful in an unconventional way with ease and grace by reading the strategies written in the book.

My mission with this book was to serve you and make a positive difference in your life by inspiring you to think, feel and act differently.

My hope is that you have become more inspired and empowered to follow **"The Unconventional Way to Wealth".**

Whether you achieve your dreams or goals is solely up to you. Only you have the power to promise or guarantee what level of success you will achieve in your life.

However, by following these 5 steps to **"Be Extraordinary Wealthy"** explained in this book, YOU CAN begin to achieve your desire in no distant future. No matter where you are.

YOU CAN DO IT - THE TIME TO START IS NOW!

Again, congratulations!

"Good Things Come to Those Who
Go Out and Grab Them."

Acknowledgements

Through the years, many have shared ideas, mentoring and support that has impacted my life, each in a different way. Please know that I appreciate you greatly.

I acknowledge with joy and pleasure.

First and foremost, I would like to bow to Lord Shiva, Shakti and the entire family for all the blessings I am fortunate to have in my life! I believe that this book is a blessing to me from Higher Authorities.

An outstanding group of people have come together to make this book possible. Without them this would have never been possible. And I would like to thank them all.

Special Gratitude must go:

To My Husband Mr. Chirag Kansal for his love, support and presence around me.

To My Parents Mr. Satish Goyal & Ms. Kamla Goyal for giving me birth and providing their support at every step of my life.

To My Extended In-laws family for their presence in my life.

To My Siblings and their respective families Rita - Rajesh, Rinki-Mukesh, Shalini-Dinesh, Vineet-Mamta, Naveen-Kalpana, for always being there with me and encouraging me through the entire year of this long project.

To All my nieces, nephews, cousins, uncles, aunts, maternal & paternal friends and family for their loving presence in my life.

To my publisher and entire team of Beeja House, led by Geetika Saigal including, Apoorva Khare, Saakshi Kaushal and Shristy, for sharing a dream with me.

To Inspiring Indian Women who became my role models of Women Empowerment - Aishwarya Rai Bachchan, Priyanka Chopra Jonas, Alia Bhatt Kapoor.

To my Invisible mentors Savitri Simpson, Louise Hay, Abraham Hicks, Sadhguru, James Malinchak, Dan Lok. To My Visible Mentors Shilpa Singh and Sami Wunder.

To My wonderful readers who have shown their loving support for my work and for the leap of faith in picking up the book of a debut author.

And lastly, to my dear childhood friends Rakesh, Poonam, Preeti & Shalini who surrounded me with love, laughter, and lots of fun!

Thank You.

About the Author

REETU GOYAL KANSAL

Reetu Goyal Kansal had a pretty successful career in banking. For 11+ years. she worked with private banks but when she found herself forgetting her desires and dreams in favour of being accepted, making it up the ranks and fitting in, she realised that this traditional way of doing, achieving and actioning is not leading her anywhere but left her feeling empty, completely disconnected and questioning her existence as a Human Being?

This made her conscious of investing her time, energy and money in her personal growth and self-development. She took this new path towards self-discovery and what she discovered is this unknown, unexplored realm of the **"Inner World ",** *where she not only found her authority back, but she also found the most unique and fulfilling ways to wealth and success within only.*

She decided to quit her job. And now she spends most of her time inspiring, empowering and enabling others to invest in themselves and in their beautiful future through her unconventional programs like, The Unconditioned You, Unlock Your Wealth Potential, her book - The Unconventional Way to Wealth, Membership Programs like Conscious Creator's, Create Consciously, Personal Coaching & 1-2-1 Mentoring, Webinars, Conscious Creator's YouTube Video and Much More.

Reetu is a leading Wealth Consciousness coach and Feminine/ Masculine Energy Expert, who is now on a mission to help people to break free from the conventional ways of doing things, unlearn social conditioning to create wealth and success in more unique and fulfilling ways.

Her only desire now is to see people thriving in all areas of life, being financially free, doing what they love to do.

You can also be a part of her exclusive Facebook Group - Conscious Creator's, to receive free daily insights about creating wealth consciously and effortlessly.

And this book will show you exactly what is needed to build a wealthy, purposeful and fulfilled life.

Additional Resources
Online Course Order Page

To help you to become a high value individual, achieve more success and to create infinite income, influence and impact there are

FREE BONUS RESOURCES AND OPPORTUNITY

TO BOOK A STRATEGY SESSION for you at:
www.reetugoyalkansal.com

Free guide to heal and get familiar with your feminine & masculine energies.

To order go to:

www.reetugoyalkansal.com

Special FREE Bonuses and Gifts for You

Dear Readers, I thank you for choosing to read this book!

Now, I want to reward you for finishing this book. Here is how you can win gifts like free webinar seat worth Rs. 6999 ($100), free recorded courses starting from Rs. 14999($200), free personality test worth Rs. 14999 ($200), free strategy session worth Rs. 49999 ($690), private group access. You have to move these 2 steps to become eligible to win some gifts:

Move 1 *- Share your review of this book on Amazon and Goodreads because this will help me to reach more people who are ready to break-free from the never-ending hustle of the traditional world to create wealth and success in more unique and fulfilling ways. Please send me the screenshot of it at the contact details given on the last page. Either Facebook or Email.*

Move 2 *- Share your key learnings from the book on social media, tag me and 2 of your best friends who must read this book. Use the tag*

#TheUnconventionalWayToWealth.

I am happy that you have finished the book but that is not my end goal. Nothing will make me happier than seeing you creating wealth consciously and effortlessly, by implementing the principles & strategies shared in the book.

I would love to see and hear your success stories. Please do share with me from time to time and I may give you a shout - out or even meet you personally if the time permits. Do share the proof of your success story.

I also want you to insist at least 2 of your best friends or family members who you care for the most to read this book. There is no better gift than giving someone the tools for creating wealth and success effortlessly.

If you want to join our group then you can go to Facebook and join the group called "Conscious Creator's" (By Reetu Goyal Kansal). I share a lot of my secrets in these groups from time to time for free!

Thank You For having me as your Wealth Consciousness Coach and I look forward to connecting with you on social media and in person as well someday!

Connect With the Author

If you want to continue to learn how to implement these strategies further, if you want to be a part of the Conscious Creator's family then do reach out to us.

We will help you to create your life consciously and with least resistance.

Website: www.reetugoyalkansal.com
Email: support@reetugoyalkansal.com
Instagram: www.instagram.com/reetugoyalkansal/
LinkedIn: www.linkedin.com/in/reetugoyalkansal
Facebook Group: www.facebook.com/ groups/ 247 845131421549/

I have been inspired by the higher authorities to write this book and I would be grateful to help you become a high value individual who is now inspired to create infinite income, influence and impact!

References

Part 1

10 Ways to Get the Best ROI on Your Self-Development Practices | Inc.com

Personal Growth: The Challenge and Value of Finding Your Own Way | HuffPost Life

How to Become a High-Value Person | by Colin Zhang | Change Your Mind Change Your Life | Medium

How to Invest in Yourself - Choose Yourself | SELF MADE (becomingselfmade.com)

Part 2

Lousie Hay - You Can Heal Your Life

Savitri Simpson - Chakras for Starters

Abraham Hicks: The 5 Steps to Alignment

Savitri Simpson - Through the Chakras: A Tale of Adventure in the Seven Golden Pyramids

Part 3

5 myths about living a life of passion,purpose & profit - debunked - www.hareker.com

Neville Goddard - Feeling Is The Secret, The power of Awareness

Mindset – Make Money by Adding Value – Conscious Millionaire

"The Coin of Heaven" – Neville Goddard lecture transcript – Max Harrick Shenk, writer (wordpress.com)

www.ingramcontent.com/pod-product-compliance
Lightning Source LLC
Chambersburg PA
CBHW021214250926
51852CB00006B/1
9789395266956